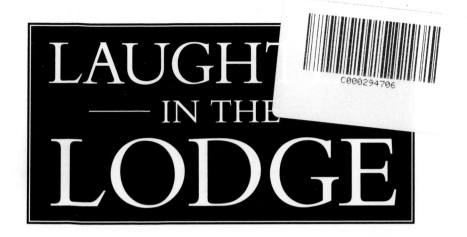

LAUGHTER
— IN THE
LODGE

Steve Chadburn

Lewis Masonic

This impression 2013

ISBN 978 0 85318 481 2

Published by Lewis Masonic

an imprint of Ian Allan Publishing Ltd, Hersham, Surrey KT12 4RG.

Printed in England

Distributed in the United States of America and Canada by BookMasters Distribution Services

Visit the Lewis Masonic website at *www.lewismasonic.co.uk*

DEDICATION
I'd like to dedicate this book to my Mother Lodge, The Leicestershire and Rutland Rotary Lodge 9158 and the wellbeing of all my brothers and friends therein.

See more of Steve's work at *http://www.steve-chadburn.com/*

You need many fine attributes to be a Freemason…
a thick skin can also be useful

My inspiration……

Cartoonists are by instinct and experience professional people watchers and I hope you will find my observations of Freemasons both interesting and amusing. I've tried to cover all aspects of involvement in the Craft and how we manage to balance the increasingly complicated demands on our time from work and families in the modern world, with our philosophy of universal Brotherhood.

To me, Freemasonry has been a personal journey of self-discovery from Apprentice to Past Master, where words like 'integrity' and 'personal honour' now have meaning but in the learning there has also been fun and fellowship; an oasis of harmony to recharge my batteries in a changing world.

In expressing my ideas I've tried to cover facets not often illustrated but you'll find no secrets, so please don't hold your breath looking. Just enjoy, there is something here to make you smile.

Kind regards,
Steve

The evolution of a modern Mason…

…but we've probably been around a lot longer

Freemasonry is not a religion

but attracts people of moral worth

People are fascinated by our secrets…

it's in the summons
as a demonstration…

they think we get up to the strangest things!

There is no doubt we are easier to spot these days…

Wife says we should have a more obvious public profile…

…with a little help

Embalmers night class, Madam

But we still keep our sense of humour

They must have something to hide…they wouldn't let us in

People however, still get the wrong idea

So where we can, we've adopted a more open attitude…

They are for supporting my chin Madam,
when I get tired of answering stupid questions

...this openness has its critics

Think we may be overdoing it?

Who's going to tell him it's upside down?

The meeting where everybody brought a guest…

...could cause problems finding your case

**Freemasons love to visit other Lodges – a stranger
is just a Brother you haven't met before**

**When visiting other Lodges, it is interesting
to see slight variations of the ritual**

Welcome to the Migraine Lodge

Traditions in other Lodges can be based on many factors

The Lodge was founded by Veterinary Surgeons

occupations used to be popular

Sometimes the Master will have his own ideas…

... you could continue the football theme

No, it isn't ritual – the W.M. has dropped his mints

Traditions may start in the strangest of ways

**We like to preserve our traditions but we hardly
ever blindfold the cleaner these days**

**Lodges have many key and respected characters
– the Treasurer being one of them**

The Secretary is another, providing he keeps his announcements to the basic facts

Organists have been known
to be a little eccentric…

…some have learnt to play
at the Les Dawson School
of Music

He's here now, always leaves
him with a smile on his face

The Almoner keeps an eye on the sick and infirm

Tyler's duties involve spending time on their own…

…they can get bored

**It is not unknown for prospective clients
to view the hospitality facilities**

**It's worth noting that the Tyler can also be
the first point of contact with the public**

The Deacons are the workhorses of any Lodge

The Prompter, who hangs on every word

He's teaching me a tracing board

Every Lodge has its own approach to learning ritual…

...but it needs to be done with feeling

**Masons will try not to let illness prevent
them attending Lodge**

For every Freemason, the day will come when he receives his copy of the ritual book

This then becomes his constant companion – to the exclusion of everything else

One should take every opportunity to brush up

Practising in the car is popular...

...and the dog can make a good and confidential audience

All Master Masons are encouraged to attend rehearsals on time, except sometimes the key holder

Rehearsals help reinforce the harmony of the Lodge

The Director of Ceremonies is easy to spot at rehearsals…

…as is the Assistant Director of Ceremonies

**Sometimes rehearsals are complicated by an inability of the
House Committee to remember to schedule the heating**

We want you to sell it on eBay

The problem can be complicated by a pedigree dating back to Elias Ashmole

Lodges are often blessed with visits by senior Freemasons looking like graduates from the Masonic Charm School

George… you've been practicing your look of
Provincial disapproval again, haven't you?

Senior Freemasons have always had their portraits done…

… with varying degrees of enthusiasm

**It's fair to say that a lot of Masons find Side Degrees
a little confusing…**

What exactly was the brief we gave her?

**... so good communications matter – especially
with the lady designing your new Lodge banner**

About these new safety regulations…

**Freemasonry has a broad back when it comes
to pressure for change…**

...sponsorship may become possible, even welcomed...

… but do get one that's relevant

Regalia outlets may well stock the latest in gadgets…

This tracing board doubles as a sun bed in the close season

... some more useful than others

Think I preferred signing my name in a big leather book

Barcodes may become the order of the day

Remember to turn your phone off… even if it is on vibrate…

Lodges however, will usually find their own way of preserving traditions and curbing the introduction of new technology

Psssssst, want to be a Freemason??

People get the wrong idea on how you join us

It is usually friends or family who may approach you, although these days it's possible to seek advice and information from your local Provincial team

If interest is shown, usually an informal gathering will initially discuss with you what is required and answer any questions

**There are certain requirements which you
as an individual must meet**

It's important to discuss it with your wife, if you have one…

… but don't get talked into a leg wax!

**When eventually you enter the Lodge for the first time,
take it on trust and enjoy a truly memorable experience**

It's likely you will be appointed a mentor, who will guide you an all sorts of topics. Like when to wear your apron… and when not to

You may witness the odd mistake from time to time, which all adds to the experience…

... and gives you a thirst for the bar at the end of the meeting

You must be the Morris dancers?

**Assuming the House Committee haven't double booked
the facilities…again**

It is usually the Chief Steward who liaises with the caterers to ensure the Festive Board runs smoothly without problems

Occasionally things may not run smoothly…

…Prepared whilst the Chef was drunk

**Another Lodge's Festive Board can be both an experience…
and an adventure**

We believe in keeping our Stewards busy

Like in the ceremony, they can have their funny little ways

**Festive Boards can take their toll…
the first meeting of the Masonic year
is a good test of your waistline…**

...or...problem, what problem?

As Master, beware of the Brother who wants just a couple of minutes to mention something like a Masonic golf gathering…

**...that two minutes is bound to last longer
than a tracing board**

Poor speakers never know when to shut up

The harmony of the Lodge should extend to your family life

Summer events are a good way of strengthening bonds between family and Lodge

Skittles evenings are popular with the ladies

Maybe it's all just an elaborate chess game...

Involving your family has its merits...

I now invest you with the apron of a washer upper

… as well as its hazards

*Something about free and
not operative…*

We do have our funny little ways…

I know what they are…AND what they do!
Just get on with it!

…the subtlety of which can be missed

*…says it's all part
of being a new age
sensitive Mason…*

Be prepared to do your share of the work…

… but I draw the line at the ironing

The Worshipful Master and his even more WORSHIPFUL LADY!

The Ladies' Festival is our way of saying 'Thank you'

As it's OUR evening, I thought I'd let him do the driving for a change

I hear it's a lighter than usual Masonic repast..?

Who ordered the Chicken Seizure?

**Getting the right menu from the usual Masonic
heavy duty Festive Board can be tricky**

It's his 'Goat Stranglers' evening

**Support from your good lady would make life easier…
and avoid the odd barbed comment**

You're a most Excellent what...??

Freemasons work hard in the name of Charity

Province can be relied upon to offer suggestions

No, you pay him NOT to show you the tattoo!

As individuals and teams, Freemasons will work
and support any worthy cause they are able to

**Some areas of fund-raising might be considered
not quite the thing to do…**

However, the Charity Steward will probably get a second helping at the Festive Board

**In our modern world, the older you get the more
unimportant and invisible you seem to become**

One of the things I have noted and cherished about Freemasonry is the way people are not diminished by age